Little Red Riding Hood

A Parragon Book

Published by
Parragon Books,
Unit 13–17, Avonbridge Trading Estate,
Atlantic Road, Avonmouth, Bristol BS11 9QD

Produced by
The Templar Company plc,
Pippbrook Mill, London Road, Dorking, Surrey RH4 1JE

Designed by Mark Kingsley-Monks

Printed and bound in Italy

ISBN 0-75250-924-1

Little Red Riding Hood

Retold by Caroline Repchuk
Illustrated by Martin Aitchinson

‖ •PARRAGON• ‖

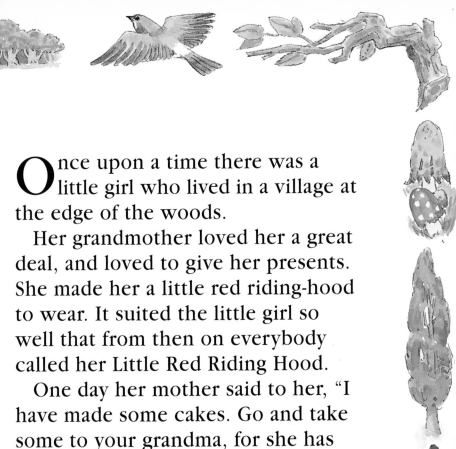

Once upon a time there was a little girl who lived in a village at the edge of the woods.

Her grandmother loved her a great deal, and loved to give her presents. She made her a little red riding-hood to wear. It suited the little girl so well that from then on everybody called her Little Red Riding Hood.

One day her mother said to her, "I have made some cakes. Go and take some to your grandma, for she has not been well and it would make her so happy to see you."

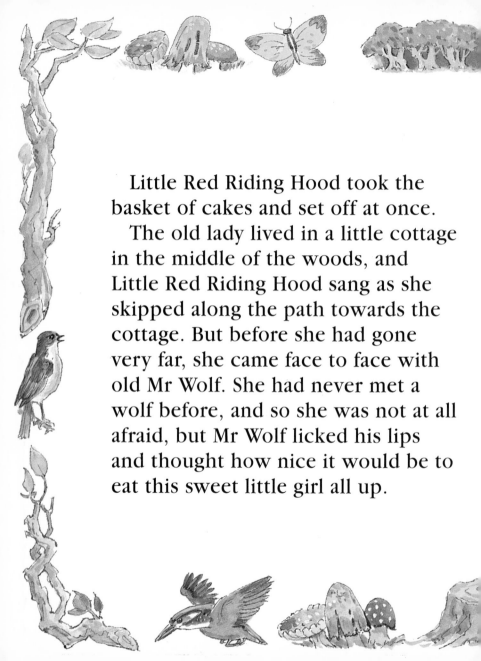

Little Red Riding Hood took the basket of cakes and set off at once.

The old lady lived in a little cottage in the middle of the woods, and Little Red Riding Hood sang as she skipped along the path towards the cottage. But before she had gone very far, she came face to face with old Mr Wolf. She had never met a wolf before, and so she was not at all afraid, but Mr Wolf licked his lips and thought how nice it would be to eat this sweet little girl all up.

"Good day, my pretty," said the Wolf. "And where are you going on this fine sunny morning?"

"I am going to visit my grandma," the little girl replied politely.

"Where does she live?" asked the cunning Wolf.

"In the little cottage right in the middle of the wood," answered Little Red Riding Hood.

"Well," said the Wolf, "I think I'll go and see her too. I'll go this way, and you go that way, and we shall see who gets there first."

Then the Wolf began to run as fast as he could along the quickest path, and the little girl went the long way round, down the prettiest path.

She didn't hurry, but stopped to chase after butterflies, and pick the pretty wild flowers that covered the ground.

Soon the Wolf arrived outside the old woman's cottage. Peeking through the window he could see the plump little old lady tucked up snuggly in bed. She looked rather tasty too. He knocked at the door — tap, tap, tap.

"Who's there?" came a little shaky voice from inside.

"It is I, Grandma, Little Red Riding Hood," replied the Wolf, copying the little girl's high squeaky voice. "I have brought you some cakes and a pot of good butter from my mother."

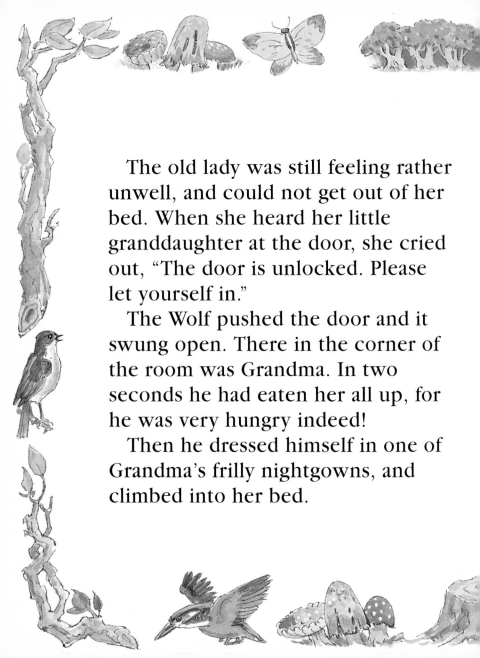

The old lady was still feeling rather unwell, and could not get out of her bed. When she heard her little granddaughter at the door, she cried out, "The door is unlocked. Please let yourself in."

The Wolf pushed the door and it swung open. There in the corner of the room was Grandma. In two seconds he had eaten her all up, for he was very hungry indeed!

Then he dressed himself in one of Grandma's frilly nightgowns, and climbed into her bed.

It wasn't long before Little Red Riding Hood was gently knocking at the door — tap, tap, tap.

"Who's there?" called out the Wolf, in a little shaky voice. Little Red Riding Hood thought Grandma sounded a little gruffer than usual, but decided she must have a sore throat from her illness. She called out:

"It is I, Grandma, Little Red Riding Hood. I have brought you some cakes from my mother."

"The door is open, come inside, dear," called the Wolf.

Little Red Riding Hood opened the door and stepped inside.

"Come and sit by me, my dear," said the Wolf.

Little Red Riding Hood was amazed to see how ill and peculiar her grandmother looked.

"Oh, Grandma, what big ears you have!" she said.

"All the better to hear you with, my dear," replied the Wolf.

"And what big eyes you have!"

"All the better to see you with, my dear."

"And what big teeth you have!"

"All the better to eat you with!" and the wicked Wolf gobbled down Little Red Riding Hood in one mouthful.

Now his belly was very full indeed and with a big yawn, the Wolf climbed back into bed and was soon snoring loudly.

Not long after this a tired woodcutter was returning home through the wood. He passed close by the cottage and decided to call in on Little Red Riding Hood's grandmother, for he had heard that she was ill.

He knocked loudly at the door, and became rather worried when there was no reply. Then, as he stood and listened, he heard the sound of snoring coming from inside.

"She must be asleep," he thought to himself. "I'll just pop my head around the door and check that she is alright."

But as he opened the door and stepped inside, what a sight met his eyes!

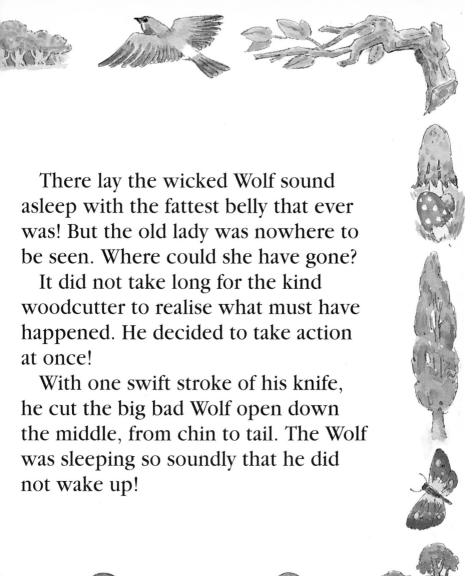

There lay the wicked Wolf sound asleep with the fattest belly that ever was! But the old lady was nowhere to be seen. Where could she have gone?

It did not take long for the kind woodcutter to realise what must have happened. He decided to take action at once!

With one swift stroke of his knife, he cut the big bad Wolf open down the middle, from chin to tail. The Wolf was sleeping so soundly that he did not wake up!

Then out jumped Little Red Riding Hood.

"Oh, thank you kindly!" she cried. "It was so hot in there that I could hardly breathe!"

Together Little Red Riding Hood and the woodcutter pulled Grandma out from the Wolf's stomach and laid her gently on the bed to rest, for such an experience had not aided her recovery one little bit.

She was delighted to see her dear little granddaughter at last.

The Wolf was still snoring loudly, as he lay fast asleep on the floor.

Then the woodcutter went to fetch some large stones from the forest.

He filled the Wolf's belly to the brim, then sewed the cut tight and they hid in the corner to see what would happen next.

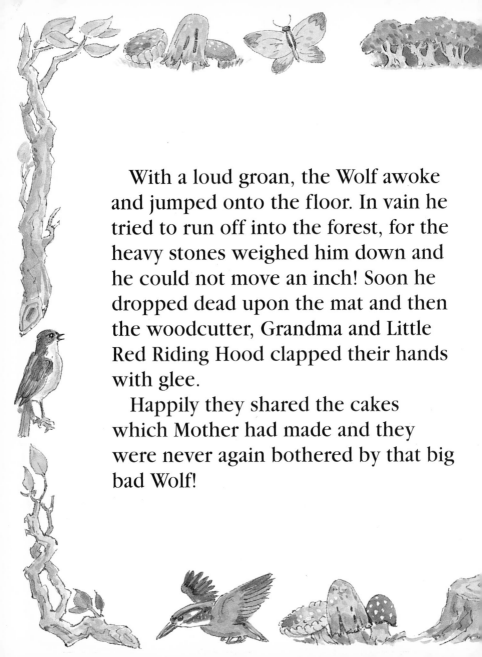

With a loud groan, the Wolf awoke and jumped onto the floor. In vain he tried to run off into the forest, for the heavy stones weighed him down and he could not move an inch! Soon he dropped dead upon the mat and then the woodcutter, Grandma and Little Red Riding Hood clapped their hands with glee.

Happily they shared the cakes which Mother had made and they were never again bothered by that big bad Wolf!

CHARLES PERRAULT

Little Red Riding Hood first appeared
in print in 1697 in the collection of fairy stories
written by the French poet and storyteller,
Charles Perrault (1628-1703).
He brought together many half-forgotten folk
tales such as *Cinderella*, *Bluebeard* and *Puss in
Boots* and over the years they became popular
throughout the world.
Little Red Riding Hood originally ended with the
wolf pouncing on the little girl but the Brothers
Grimm added the ending we have here,
with a woodcutter rescuing both Red Riding
Hood and her grandmother.

The Three Billy Goats Gruff is a Norwegian
folk tale collected by Asbjørnsen and Moe.
In Norse mythology the goat is sacred to the
god Thor and drew his chariot. The trolls lived in
great fear of Thor so it was most fitting that a
goat got the better of the troll in this story.